PEMBROKESHIRE COAST HIGH

PEMBROKESHIRE COAST HIGH

AN AERIAL JOURNEY

SKYWORKS

HALSGROVE

First published in Great Britain in 2007

British Library Cataloguing-in-Publication Data
A CIP record for this title is available from the British Library

ISBN 978 1 84114 683 6

HALSGROVE
Halsgrove House
Ryelands Industrial Estate
Bagley Road, Wellington
Somerset TA21 9PZ
Tel: 01823 653777
Fax: 01823 216796
email: sales@halsgrove.com
website: www.halsgrove.com

Printed and bound by D'Auria Industrie Grafiche Spa, Italy

Introduction

Jutting out into the Atlantic as though to guard the entrance to Wales, the 260-mile long Pembrokeshire coast is among the most beautiful in Europe. It was deservedly given National Park status in 1952, and today is visited by an estimated five million people a year. There are over fifty beaches, several islands – of which Skomer has the largest grey seal colony in Southern Britain and one of only two Marine Nature Reserves in the country – and, in St David's, the smallest city in Britain. Several tiny fishing villages hug the coastline, but at Milford Haven, one of the most outstanding deep-water harbours in the world, colossal supertankers are regular visitors bringing oil to the refinery at Rhoscrowther. Tenby, meanwhile, still retains the character of a handsome Georgian seaside resort.

For all its apparent serenity today, the Pembrokeshire coast has had an occasionally turbulent past. Its accessible position on the sea lanes opened it up from ancient times not only to trade from far distant ports, but also to invasion over the centuries. The Vikings landed, sacked and settled, leaving – among other things – Norse names for the islands. The Normans occupied South Pembrokeshire, so easily reached from the sea, and built a line of castles that eventually divided Pembrokeshire into the wilder, 'Welsh' north and the gentler, 'English' south, a partition that is still reflected in the area's language and customs. Nearer our own day, the last invasion of the British mainland occurred at Carregwasted Point near Fishguard in 1797, when Napoleon's troops attempted an attack but were repulsed (so legend has it) by formidable Welsh matrons wearing traditional black hats and red cloaks.

Other invasions have been altogether friendlier. Celtic monks from Ireland spread Christianity originally. Then Saint David, the patron saint of Wales, established a monastery in the sixth century where he was buried in 588; enlarged and rebuilt, this is today the magnificent St David's Cathedral. In our own time the spirit of the Celtic saints survives, with the Cistercian monks of Caldey Abbey offering a friendly welcome to the many travellers who take the short crossing from Tenby.

Some visitors come to the Pembrokeshire coast for more physical reasons. St David's is a significant centre for adventure sports, particularly surfing and climbing, whilst the cliffs around the southern coast are some of the most popular sea-cliff climbing locations in Britain. But others come just for the walking and the views, and the spiritual refreshment that this area can bring. It offers vistas of staggering variety, from peaceful estuaries to wave-tossed shores, wild moorland to oak-fringed rivers, sandy beaches to astonishing cliffs, all of them shown in a fascinating perspective in this aerial tour around the coast. Somehow from the skies you also gain a deeper sense of the almost other-worldly nature of this landscape. Pembrokeshire was anciently called 'the land of mystery and enchantment' and much of that still remains.

SKYWORKS

For aerial shots with impact, look no further…

Skyworks is an independent television production company and a stock footage library specialising in top-end High Definition filming from the air. The company has become one of the world's leading HD aerial archives for High Definition video and stills.

Skyworks is creatively led by Richard Mervyn, the world's most experienced aerial cameraman/producer/director. He works with specially trained film pilots, purpose-rigged helicopters and the most advanced aerial camera systems in order to produce footage of the highest quality.

The Skyworks' team is systematically travelling the globe and filming locations in the unique style for which the company has become renowned. Skyworks' archive collection is already geographically broad and thematically diverse. The company's vision is to continue filming until the world has been covered and catalogued for all to see.

On the television side, Skyworks produces a range of factual programmes, varying from series about history, landscape and heritage to observational documentaries and more recently drama-documentary. Skyworks has produced over 100 factual programmes for international broadcasters, including the BBC, Discovery and ITV.

Skyworks is constantly expanding its product base, as the company becomes synonymous with high class aerial imagery – however and wherever it is used.

In the future, everyone in the world will be able to access Skyworks' content, put together in a variety of engaging and informative ways, allowing them to explore the globe from the comfort of their armchair.

www.skyworks.co.uk

The Preseli Hills form the largest inland area of the Pembrokeshire Coast National Park. The Park is the only one in Britain to be predominantly coastal in character: nowhere is more than 10 miles from the sea.

The highest point in the Preseli Hills (and, indeed, Pembrokshire) is Foel Cwmcerwyn at 1760ft (536m).

The landscape of the Preseli Hills is in many places more reminiscent
of Dartmoor than this corner of Wales.

The tops of the Preseli have an air of myth and mystery that invests 'real' ancient sites with legend: connections with King Arthur are particularly popular.

One association is geologically proven: that the Preseli Hills are the source of the bluestones from which Stonehenge is constructed. How they got to Wiltshire, however, is a matter of long conjecture.

Heading towards the coast with Abercastle in the middle distance.

Myndd Morfa and Pen-yr-allt Wood on the left, with coastal farms in the centre.

Mynydd Morfa on the right and the rocky headland of Ynys Deullyn stretching out on the left.

Looking north west over Pen-yr-allt Wood towards Penbwchdy.
The sandy beach of Aber Mawr lies invitingly in the centre.

Over the brow of Myndd Morfa. The Pembrokeshire Coast Path hugs the bay.

Ynys Deullyn and Ynys y Castell guard the secretive little harbour of Abercastle.

Abercastle peeps in to view. Longhouse, top left, is the site of a prehistoric cromlech.

Cwm Badau, the Valley of the Boats, at Abercastle is first mentioned in the 1500s as a safe harbour.

Picturesque in summer, Abercastle has been an essential
haven for seamen against fierce winter gales for centuries.

Looking south west, towards the headland at Trwyn Llwyd in the centre and the cliffs around Porthgain beyond.

The outskirts of the village of Trefin can be seen, lying inland on the left.
Trefin once had a reputation as a centre for smuggling.

The point at Trwyn Llwyd.

The line of the Pembrokeshire Coast Path skirts the cliff edge at Trwyn Llwyd. This National Trail follows the coastline of the Pembrokeshire Coast National Park for 186 miles (299km).

Overlooking the point at Trwyn Llwyd. The sharp and jagged rocks emphasise the danger this coastline could pose to mariners in rough seas.

The outcrop of Ynys-fach lies in the centre with the headland of Trwyn Elen above it.

As with many locations on this coast, the sea has carved caves into Ynys-fach. Cave exploration by sea-kayak is a popular adventure activity on the Pembrokeshire Coast.

Trwyn Elen on the right, Porthgain hidden in its cwm behind.

Porthgain was an important slate-quarrying and exporting centre up to the 1930s.
Later stone-quarrying and brick-making took over.

Above Porthgain's harbour are the remains of the storage hoppers from which crushed stone was loaded into waiting ships.

Today, with the decline of industry, Porthgain harbour is used by pleasure boats and lobster fishermen.

'Sculpted' cliffs to the west above Porthgain.

Pen Porth Egr, immediately to the west of Porthgain.

The Bay of Traeth Llyfn with the Cerrig Gwylan rocks on the right and
Trwyncastell marking the other side of its mouth on the left.

Looking over into Abereiddi Bay, with the waves lapping the sandy shore. Once a slate-quarrying centre, Abereiddi is now little more than a few houses.

Abereiddi Bay. Abandoned quarries around this area of coast tell a story of industrial decline in the twentieth century. The so called 'Blue Lagoon' here at Abereiddi (bottom centre) is actually a drowned quarry.

Looking south west towards St David's Head. Trwyn Aber-pwll and Stacan Barcutan lie in the middle distance.

Along with the relics of extractive industries, the coast also boasts
a number of prehistoric sites like the Caerau hillforts (centre left).

As the Pembrokeshire Coast Path skirts the sea cliffs it is possible to
gaze down into millions of years' worth of exposed geology.

Slightly further west are the remains of the Castell Coch hillfort.

The Ynys Gwair rock and, further out, the detached Carreg-gwylan-fach.

Carn Penberry rises to the left above Penclegyr and Trwyn Dduallt.

An (almost) walkers'-eye view of the cliff edge (detail).

The great hill of Carn Llidi rises up on Saint David's Head, with Ramsey Island visible beyond.

The point at Penllechwen juts out into the sea on the top right.

Carn Llidi (left) is 593ft (181m) high and offers tremendous views.
Below it are the traces of prehistoric field systems with walls 2000 years old.

Whitesands Bay, with Ramsey Island to the left of Carn Llidi.

Whitesands Bay has one of the finest stretches of sandy beaches in Pembrokeshire.
It is said to be from here that St Patrick embarked for Ireland.

Ramsey Island sustains one of the largest grey seal colonies in Britain. The island's two hills are Carnysgubor on the right and Carnllundain in the middle of this view.

Ramsey Sound with the little harbour of St Justinian's at the bottom.

St Justinian's is named for Justinian, a monk on Ramsey Island whose followers rebelled and cut off his head. Nothing daunted Justinian picked up his head and carried it ashore here.

The ruins of a late medieval chapel dedicated to St Justinian are one of the few sights in the port.

The lifeboat house at St Justinian's. A ferry runs from here to Ramsey Island in the summer.

Carn ar Wig, Penmaen melyn and Pen Dal-aderyn on the mainland,
looking across the narrowest point of Ramsey Sound.

The name of The Bitches rocks, off Ramsey Island, tell all about the fear
and frustration these treacherous waters arouse in mariners.

Rounding Pont Ynys-bery, Ramsey Island.

Passing through the roaring waters of Ramsey Sound, notorious for its currents and rip tides.

Bay Dillyn, Ramsey Island, looking north to the hill of Carnllundain.

At the southern end of Ramsey Island a boat speeds past Ynys Cantwr and Twll y Gwyddel.

The rounded form of Ynys Gwelltog at the foot of Ramsey Island.

Looking north over Ramsey Sound to St David's Head.

Over Ramsey Island to its northern hill Carnysgubor.

The large Ynys Eilun rock and its companion Pont yr Eilun.

The base of the St David's peninsula, looking north towards St David's Head.

Carreg Frân rocks.

Carreg Frân looking over to the Carreg yr Esgob skerries.

The sea crashes dramatically over Carreg Frân.

Calmer waters in Porth Henllys.

The twin beaches at Porthlysgi Bay.

Heading inland towards St David's.

St David's (Ty Ddewi) was established when David, patron saint of Wales,
built a monastery here in the sixth century.

St David's is the smallest city in Britain – of village size, it was granted official city status by the Queen in 1995.

Unlike many cathedrals, St David's is hidden in a hollow, a location chosen to protect it from Viking raiders.

St David's Cathedral was founded in 550AD, but the present
building was begun by Bishop Peter de Leia in 1180.

In the Cathedral Close (bottom) are the ruins of the thirteenth-century
Bishop's Palace and the restored College of St Mary.

Caerfai Bay, a little to the south of St David's, on the broad expanse of St Brides Bay.

Looking down to the sands of Caerfai Bay.

The view down to Caerfai beach enjoyed by walkers on the Pembrokeshire Coast Path.

Sea caves along the coast south of Trelerw.

The Cradle and Segar Rock, bottom right, with Solva creeping in to view on the left.

The harbour of Solva, one of the safest on this coast, was hidden from the gaze of pirates.

Solva is effectively divided into two: Lower Solva at the head of the inlet and Upper Solva on the left above the harbour. The little beach of Gwadn can be seen on the right.

Porth Gwyn, Porth y Bwch and Aber-west in the curve around to Dinas Fawr on the far right.

The long finger of Dinas Fach stretches out into St Brides Bay with the line of Newgale Sands beyond.

Just beyond Dinas Fach lies the secluded cove of Porthmynawyd.

A closer view of the craggy promontory of Dinas Fach.

The northern edge of Newgale Sands which stretch south for some 2 miles.

Cwm Mawr on the left leading up from Newgale Sands to Penycwm.
On the right is the little settlement of Newgale.

Newgale's golden sands are backed by a storm ridge of shingle.

At very low tide or with a shifting of the sands, traces of a submerged forest are revealed at Newgale.

Newgale Sands are popular for surfing and windsurfing.

Newgale sands end at Rickets Head, in the centre of the view. Just beyond lies the former coal-exporting port of Nolton Haven, then Broad Haven and Little Haven until the coast turns west and heads out towards Stack Rocks.

The oil refinery at Robeston, just above Milford Haven.

The development of Milford Haven as an oil port from the 1950s, was one of the most profound changes in the National Park since its inception in 1952.

By 1974 there were five oil terminals and four refineries on the shores of Milford Haven.

The discovery of North Sea oil meant that the focus of the oil industry moved elsewhere.
Although Milford Haven's oil trade is very considerable it is not as great as it was in the 1970s.

The broad entrance to Milford Haven between St Ann's Head and West Angle Bay.
The village of Herbrandston lies centre left.

The village of Herbrandston (pronounced Harborston) lies to the east of the Sandyhaven estuary.

The site of the former Esso oil refinery at Herbrandston with South Hook Point on its right with Stack Rock beyond. A new multi-million-pound Liquid Natural Gas storage facility is being developed here.

Herbrandston, looking out past Gelliswick Bay to the Rhoscrowther oil refinery on the south bank of the Haven.

Tanker jetties allow ships to connect direct to oil pipelines leading to the shore.

Stack Rock was built in the mid 1800s as a fort to guard the Haven and its important Naval dockyard at Pembroke.

Known as a 'Palmerston Folly', Stack Rock fort was designed as
part of the defences against potential French invasion.

A view up-channel towards Milford Haven on the left and Pembroke Dock on the right.

Between 1967 and 1970 the largest rock-dredging operation at any port in the world
was carried out at Milford Haven to enable it to accept very large vessels.

The aim of the Milford dredging was to straighten out and widen the existing channel rather than deepening it.

In 1969 the first 250,000-ton vessel to enter a British port, the Esso Scotia arrived on her maiden voyage. Today some of the biggest ships in the world – of up to 350,000 tonnes – continue to dock at Milford Haven.

The undoubted benefits that the oil industry have brought to the Pembrokeshire economy have to be balanced against the potential environmental damage – all too apparent when the Sea Empress ran aground spilling 72,000 tonnes of oil just outside the waterway.

The town of Milford Haven was founded on land owned by Sir William Hamilton. Hamilton's wife, Lady Emma, was the lover of Admiral Nelson, who visited Milford in 1802 and praised the Haven as the world's finest deep-water harbour.

Milford Haven, with Hakin on the left and Hubberston on the right.

With the decline of the fishing industry, a marina now occupies part of Milford Haven's docks.

Milford Haven's docks were once home to the sixth biggest fishing fleet in Britain.

Looking west over Milford Haven town and the Herbranston tanker jetties.

The view from Milford Haven town south west over Man of War Roads to Angle Bay.

Looking up-stream from Milford Haven Docks with the Rhoscrowther refinery jetties on the right.

Neyland lies just beyond the refinery. In the distance can be seen the Cleddau Bridge.

The Pembrokeshire Coast Path passes through this industrial landscape between the refinery on the left-hand side and the tanker jetties on the right. Pembroke Dock lies ahead on the opposite bank.

The Irish ferry leaving Pembroke bound for Rosslare.

Pembroke Dock was a mere hamlet at the beginning of the 1800s,
but grew as a Naval town, which it remained until the 1960s.

The Pembroke River on the right hand side with the town of Pembroke in the distance.

Pembroke is an ancient town where Arnulph of Montgomery built a wooden castle in 1093.

Pembroke's wooden castle was replaced with the present stone building in 1190.
It is renowned as the birthplace of the first Tudor king, Henry VII.

Caldey Island lies 3 miles (5km) across Caldey Roads from Tenby. It has been the home of a monastery since the twelfth century.

The monastery on Caldey had historically been occupied by Benedictines but since 1929
by Cistercian monks. A visit to the island and the white-robed monks is one of the
most popular trips on the Pembrokeshire Coast.

The Giltar peninsula south west of Penally, Caldey Island a little offshore to the right.

The cliffs at Giltar are composed of Carboniferous limestone.

Giltar Point.

Having rounded Giltar Point, Tenby comes in to view.

Tenby was Pembroke's first seaside resort, with Georgians and Victorians coming
to bathe in its sea water baths and off its golden sands.

Tenby's Georgian and Victorian prosperity is reflected in its wealth of fine buildings from these periods.

The harbour at Tenby offers shelter to pleasure craft, fishing boats and the Caldey Island ferry.

Castle Hill separates the harbour at Tenby from the South Beach.

Long view out over Tenby's South Beach to Giltar Point and Caldey Island.

The fifteenth-century church of St Mary at Tenby has an elegant spire some 152ft (46m) high.
Around it spreads the well-preserved medieval street pattern.

Tenby's North Beach leads down to the harbour.

Traces of the Norman Castle (left) which defended the old town remain on Castle Hill, Tenby.

St Catherine's Island and the Sker Rock, off Tenby.

Fort St Catherine, on St Catherine's Island, is part of the Victorian defences of this coastline.

Ships from Tenby traded as far afield as Spain and France in its seafaring heyday.

In the fifteenth century, Tenby was second only to Bristol as a west coast port. The medieval town walls which are such a feature of Tenby, were built to protect this trading wealth.

Tenby has two lifeboat houses: the modern one (bottom left)
and the century-old one which it replaced (to its right).

Tenby has successfully retained its historic character whilst being a popular tourist destination.

The view north east from Tenby, with Monkstone Point on the right and Saundersfoot Bay beyond.

Looking down on to the rocks and swirling seas, so typical of the Pembrokeshire Coast National Park.